Literacy in Context

Language of
Shakespeare

Rex Gibson

General editors   **Joan Ward** *and* **John O'Connor**
Literacy consultant   **Lyn Ranson**
General consultant   **Frances Findlay**

PUBLISHED BY THE PRESS SYNDICATE OF THE UNIVERSITY OF CAMBRIDGE
The Pitt Building, Trumpington Street, Cambridge, United Kingdom

CAMBRIDGE UNIVERSITY PRESS
The Edinburgh Building, Cambridge CB2 2RU, UK
40 West 20th Street, New York, NY 10011-4211, USA
10 Stamford Road, Oakleigh, VIC 3166, Australia
Ruiz de Alarcón 13, 28014 Madrid, Spain
Dock House, The Waterfront, Cape Town 8001, South Africa

http://www.cambridge.org

First published 2001

Printed in Italy by Graphicom

Typeface Delima MT 10.5pt on 12.5pt leading   *System* QuarkXPress®

A catalogue record for this book is available from the British Library

ISBN 0 521 80564 3 paperback

Prepared for publication by Pentacor PLC

Cover illustration by Brian Lee.

Illustrations by Stephen May (pp.8, 9, 10, 15, 32, 33, 56), David Shenton (pp.20, 26, 27, 38, 63), Brian Lee (pp.45, 65, 68), Linda Worrall (p.51), Samantha Bale (p.52), Mike Ogden (p.69).

ACKNOWLEDGEMENTS
The publishers gratefully acknowledge the following for permission to reproduce copyright material.

Photographs Joseph Fiennes in *Shakespeare in Love* (p.74) ref. 577 © Laurie Sparham, by permission of Ronald Grant Archives.

Introduction

- Read a piece of text
- Read it again to discover what makes it special
- Check that you understand it
- Focus on key features
- Learn about the language features and practise using them
- Plan and write your own similar piece
- Check it and redraft

Each unit in this book helps you to understand more about a particular kind of writing, learn about its language features and then work towards your own piece of writing in a similar style.

Grammar and punctuation activities, based on the extract, will improve your language skills and take your writing to a higher level.

The book at a glance

The texts

The extracts are taken from the National Curriculum reading lists. Each part of the book contains three units of extracts and activities at different levels to help you measure your progress.

Each unit includes these sections.

Purpose

This explains exactly what you will read, learn about and write.

Key features

These are the main points to note about the way the extract is written.

Language skills

These activities will improve your grammar and punctuation. They are all based on the extracts. They are organised using the Word, Sentence and Text Level Objectives of the *National Literacy Strategy Framework for Teaching English*.

Planning your own writing

This structured, step-by-step guide will help you to get started, use writing frames and then redraft and improve your work.

Teacher's Portfolio

This includes worksheets for more language practice, revision and homework. A self-assessment chart will help you to judge and record what level you have reached and to set your own targets for improvement.

Contents

Word	Sentence	Text	Activities
• Familiar words • Unusual or old words • Onomatopoeia • Vocabulary	• Lines • Alliteration	• Rhyme and rhythm • Chorus or refrain • Creating atmosphere	Write your own song or spell
• Emotive words: nouns, verbs, adjectives • Conjunctions	• Questions • Complex sentences • Sentence length	• Speaking to the audience • Active and dramatic language	Write a soliloquy for a character in a dilemma
• Vocabulary • Alliteration	• Sentence length • Similes • Metaphors	• Point of view • Reported speech, direct speech • Evasive language	Write your own story to explain what you did

Word	Sentence	Text	Activities
• Familiar and unusual words • Using the hyphen • Adjectives and nouns	• Imperatives • Alliteration • Word order	• Dramatic language • Language of the time	Create your own insults
• Nouns • Adjectives • Adjective + noun phrases	• Vocabulary • Simile • Metaphor • Personification	• Figurative language • Atmosphere, personality, speaker's intention	Create your own images
• Vocabulary, key words • Alliteration • Rhyme scheme • Pronunciation	• Punctuation • Speech repetitions	• Parody • Stage directions • Choice of audience	Listening, collecting examples Write your own parody

5

Contents

This song of winter is sung at the end of Love's Labour's Lost

A song of winter

When icicles hang by the wall,
And Dick the shepherd **blows his nail**,   *blows on his finger nails*
And Tom bears logs unto the hall,
And milk comes frozen home in pail;
When blood is nipped, and **ways be foul**,   *roads are muddy*
Then nightly sings the staring owl,
'Tu-whit, to-who!' A merry note,
While greasy Joan doth **keel** the pot   *stir*

When all aloud the wind doth blow,
And coughing drowns the **parson's saw**,   *vicar's sermon*
And birds sit brooding in the snow,
And Marian's nose looks red and raw;
When roasted **crabs** hiss in the bowl,   *crab apples*
Then nightly sings the staring owl,
'Tu-whit, tu-who!' A merry note,
While greasy Joan doth keel the pot.

3 **Key features**

Shakespeare's spells and songs:

- have a distinctive four-beat rhythm
- use repetition of words, rhymes and rhythm
- use an imaginative vocabulary to create atmosphere

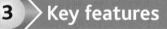

- What are the witches doing as they chant?
- How many people are mentioned in the song?
- Which creature is mentioned in both the spell and the song?

4 ▸ Language skills

Word

Shakespeare's spells and songs are filled with **familiar words**:

snake, boil, frog, icicles, log, milk...

and **unusual words** or **old words** that are no longer in use:

howlet (young owl)
saw (sermon)
crabs (crab apples)
doth keel (does stir)

❶ Find more examples in the spell and the song of unusual words or words you don't recognise. Can you guess their meaning from their context? Use a dictionary to check your guess. Write them down to use later in your own song or spell.

Sometimes Shakespeare uses **onomatopoeia**: words whose sounds echo their meaning:

bubble, hiss

❷ Write down other words in the song or spell that sound like their meaning.

❸ Think of one other spell that you already know, and one other song. Do they use unusual words and onomatopoeia? Write down any examples of each to use in your own spell and song.

Songs and spells have a four-beat rhthym.

Shakespeare uses an **appropriate vocabulary**: the right words to create the effect he wants. In the spell and song he chooses words which help build up the atmosphere of witches and winter. For example, in the song, *nipped* means painfully chilled by the cold.

❹ Write down the words and phrases that help create the atmosphere of the spell (mysterious and threatening witches) and the song (winter).

ti-TUM ti-TUM ti-TUM ti-TUM

ti-TUM ti-TUM ti-TUM ti-TUM

Sentence

All of Shakespeare's spells and song are divided into **lines**. Each line nearly always has a 'four-beat' **rhythm**. That means that there are four 'beats' (four syllables that you emphasise) in each line, like these in capitals:

> *EYE of NEWT and TOE of FROG*

1 Speak the spell and the song aloud. As you speak, emphasise the four-beat rhythm by tapping your desk or inventing some movement to accompany the four beats in each line.

When words in a line or sentence begin with the same letter it is called **alliteration**:

> *toil and trouble*
> *red and raw*

2 a What alliteration can you find in the first three lines of the witches' spell? Write it down.

   b What alliteration can you find in the song?

   c How do these examples of alliteration add to the effect of the language? (To help you answer, speak the lines aloud, emphasising the alliterative sounds, for example the D and the T in the first line of the spell.)

   d Write down all the examples of alliteration you have found.

Text

The purpose of a spell is to work some magic. A spell is mysterious and hypnotic, and rather threatening in tone. It has **strong rhymes** and is **rhythmical** and **repetitive**.

1 Speak the spell and the song, emphasising the rhymes at the end of each line. How do the rhymes help to add to the dramatic effect of the spell and the song?

Spells and songs have a **chorus** or **refrain**. These are repeated lines that begin or end each section or verse of the spell or song:

> *Double, double, toil and trouble;*
> *Fire burn, and cauldron bubble.*

2 Find the chorus of the song. How many lines does it have? What picture does the repeated chorus create in your mind?

3 Write a different chorus for the spell, using Shakespeare's chorus as a guide.

The purpose of a spell or a song is to **entertain the audience**, and **to create a mood or atmosphere**, like fear or suspense or magic for the spell

4 Choose either the spell or the song, and work out how to perform it on stage.

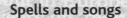

5 ▷ Planning your own writing

Shakespeare's spells and songs have much in common. They both use lively and imaginative language. They have strong and regular rhythm. Spells and songs are written to be performed on stage and to have powerful audience appeal: they almost encourage the audience to join in. And because their rhythms and rhymes are so irresistible, they are easy to memorise!

- Write your own spell or song to be chanted or sung on stage.

▶▶ STARTING POINTS

For spells:
- use Macbeth's witches as your model and invent your own ingredients
- a spell to improve your school work
- a spell for any purpose you wish

For songs
- Use the song of winter as your model and write either:
  a song of summer
  a song about holidays
  a song about school

- Write down the titles of songs you like. Alongside each title write what the song is about. Then choose one of those topics as the subject for your own song

▶▶ CLUES FOR SUCCESS

- Invent a very rhythmical chorus of two or three lines.
- Use strong rhymes.
- Ensure each line makes sense on its own.
- Use imaginative and lively words that are appropriate to the atmosphere you wish to create.
- Include onomatopoeia – words that sound like their meaning (*thump*, *clang*, *hiss*).

▶▶ REDRAFTING AND IMPROVING

Work with another student. Read each other's spells or songs. Can you make suggestions for changes by:
- adding extra lines?
- checking spellings and punctuation?
- improving rhymes?
- making the chorus easier to remember?

>> **WRITING FRAMES**

For spells:

Use one of the following Shakespeare lines as the inspiration to begin:

    When shall we three meet again?

or   The weird sisters, hand in hand,

or   Round about the cauldron go,

or   Up and down, up and down,

or   You spotted snakes, with double tongue

For songs:

Invent your own opening line or use one of the following:

    I'll sing a song about my school,

or   Here's a song of things I like to do,

or   When every day the sun shines hot,

6 Looking back

In spells and songs:

- Each **line** has a strong 'four-beat' **rhythm**.
- Each pair of lines **rhymes**.
- There are all kinds of **repetitions**.
- The **vocabulary** is imaginative, using familiar and unfamiliar words.
- A distinct **atmosphere** or **mood** is created.
- There is an easily remembered **chorus**.

Soliloquy: alone on stage!

1 ▶ Purpose

In this unit you will:

- read a soliloquy from *Romeo and Juliet*
- learn about the language of soliloquy
- write your own soliloquy to be spoken on stage

2 ▶ Juliet's fearful thoughts

Juliet wants to be reunited with Romeo who has been banished from Verona. She has agreed to Friar Lawrence's desperate plan. If she drinks a potion prepared by the Friar, it will make her seem as if she is dead. She will be placed in the family tomb, and Romeo will come to rescue her when she wakes.

Her soliloquy tells of her fears as she wonders whether to drink the potion.

	My dismal scene I needs must act alone.	
	Come, **vial**.	*small bottle (with poison)*
	What if this mixture do not work at all?	
	Shall I be married then tomorrow morning?	
5	No, no! **This** shall forbid it. Lie thou there.	*her dagger*
	What if it be a poison which the Friar	
	Subtly hath **ministered** to have me dead,	*secretly prepared*
	Lest in this marriage he should be dishonoured,	
	Because he married me before to Romeo?	
10	I fear it is, and yet methinks it should not,	
	For he hath **still** been tried a holy man.	*always*
	How if, when I am laid into the tomb,	
	I wake before the time that Romeo	
	Come to **redeem** me? There's a fearful point!	*rescue*
15	Shall I not then be stifled in the vault,	
	To whose foul mouth no healthsome air breathes in,	
	And there die strangled ere my Romeo comes?	

14

Or if I live, is it not very like

The horrible **conceit** of death and night,   *imagining*

20 Together with the terror of the place,

As in a vault, an **ancient receptacle**,   *old burying-place*

Where for this many hundred years the bones

Of all my buried ancestors are packed;

Where bloody Tybalt, yet but **green in earth**,   *newly buried*

25 Lies **fest'ring** in his shroud; where, as they say,   *rotting*

At some hours in the night spirits **resort**;   *visit*

Alack, alack, is it not like that I,

So early waking, what with loathsome smells,

And shrieks like **mandrakes** torn out of the earth,   *plants*

30 That living mortals hearing them run mad;

O, if I wake, shall I not be distraught,

Environèd with all these hideous fears,   *surrounded*

And madly play with my **forefathers' joints,**   *ancestors' limbs*

And pluck the mangled Tybalt from his shroud,

35 And in this rage, with some great kinsman's bone,

As with a club, dash out my desp'rate brains?

O look! Methinks I see **my cousin's** ghost   *Tybalt's*

Seeking out Romeo that did **spit** his body   *pierce*

Upon a rapier's point. Stay, Tybalt, stay!

Romeo, Romeo, Romeo! Here's drink. I drink to thee.

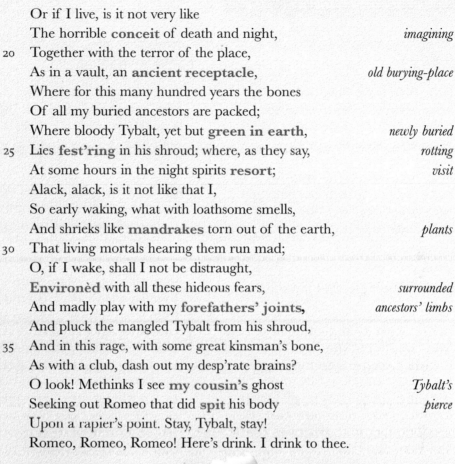

3 ⟩ Key features

Juliet's soliloquy:
- is spoken when she is alone on stage
- reveals her innermost thoughts as she considers different aspects of her situation
- uses questions and answers
- includes complex sentences

»
- What is Juliet's main emotion as she speaks?
- What does she finally decide to do?
- What is your definition of a soliloquy?

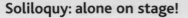

4 ▷ Language skills

Word

Juliet's soliloquy is filled with **emotive words**. Shakespeare uses emotive words when he wants to have a particular effect on the audience's feelings, or create a special atmosphere. The emotive words in Juliet's speech can help you to understand her fears about death. They include:

> **nouns:** *poison, tomb*
> **verbs:** *fear, stifled*
> **adjectives:** *fearful, foul*

1 Write down all the emotive words you can find in the soliloquy. Divide them up into three types of words: nouns, verbs and adjectives. Which type of word seems to play a greater part in creating the atmosphere of fear than the others?

As Juliet's mind moves from thought to thought, she uses many **conjunctions** to link each new thought. Conjunctions are words used to join parts of a sentence:

> *Lest* (an old way of saying unless), *because, and yet, for…*

2 Read the soliloquy quietly to yourself emphasising all the conjunctions. Choose one and write down how you think it adds to the sense of fear in Juliet's soliloquy.

Sentence

In a soliloquy a character often asks him or herself **questions**. These have a **question mark** (?) at the end of the sentence to show that it is a question.

1 How many questions does Juliet ask? To which questions does she give answers? Which questions does she only explore?

In a soliloquy, a character thinks through a problem. Their mind moves from point to point, as new thoughts come crowding in. Juliet is in a very dramatic situation, tortured by fears of what may happen to her if she drinks the potion. She moves from thought to thought, as new fears strike her. She sometimes uses **complex sentences**: sentences containing two or more clauses (parts of a sentence). In these long sentences, each clause shows a new aspect of the terror she feels.

2 The longest complex sentence is in lines 18–36. How many different things does she thinks of in this very long sentence? Count the clauses and write down a brief description of each.

Sentence length can help show what a character is feeling. Juliet's soliloquy begins with **short sentences**. As she thinks about the terrible problem she has to solve, her sentences become longer. When she makes up her mind what to do, she returns to short sentences.

Text

Shakespeare wrote soliloquies to be spoken by an actor on stage. Juliet has the choice whether to **speak directly to the audience**, or to herself, or to some thing (for example, in line 2 she may speak directly to the vial, and in line 5 to her dagger).

1 Imagine you are making a film of *Romeo and Juliet*. In a film, the director chooses what the audience will see, sometimes showing only a character's face in close-up. Work through the soliloquy line by line and suggest what the audience will see on screen at each moment.

Shakespeare's language is **active** and **dramatic language**. It is full of opportunities for physical actions and facial expressions to accompany the words. Sometimes the instructions for actions are very clearly given, for example in line 2 when Juliet says *Come, vial*, she picks up the vial and looks at it.

2 What actions does Juliet perform at lines 5 and 40?

3 Work through the whole soliloquy suggesting actions and facial expressions where you think appropriate. Present your suggestions like this:

> line 1   *looks determined; locks door of bedroom*
>
> line 2   *takes vial from under pillow*
>
> line 3   *looks worried and doubtful*
>
> line 4   *eyes widen; looks startled*

Shakespeare's **images** are sometimes based on things that modern audiences do not know. For example, in his day, it was a common belief that mandrakes (plants) grew below gallows and that when they were pulled up, they shrieked (see line 29).

4 Invent an image to replace *mandrakes torn out of the earth*. Your image should be one that a modern audience would understand.

5 ▷ Planning your own writing

In a soliloquy, a character explores a problem. The character considers different aspects of the problem and tries to find a solution. Often, all kinds of thoughts come crowding in, one thought triggering off another. At the end of the soliloquy, the character often makes a final decision.

● Invent a character who faces a particular dilemma.

● Write a soliloquy for the character as they try to work out a solution.

≫ STARTING POINTS

● A soldier has been ordered into battle where he faces almost certain death. Should he fight or run away?

● Your best friend has committed a terrible crime. Should you tell the police?

● Your soliloquy may be far less serious in tone:

 – a teenager cannot decide which dress to wear to a party

 – shall I watch TV, go to the pub, or walk the dog, or...?

≫ CLUES FOR SUCCESS

● Begin with a question. End with a decision.

● Use short sentences at first.

● Use some longer sentences to explore different thoughts that occur to the character.

● Use different conjunctions to link the character's thoughts.

● Use emotive words to create atmosphere.

WRITING FRAMES

Beginnings

Shall I .... ?

What if .... ?

Do I .... ?

Create complex sentences using conjunctions:

If..., then..., but..., or..., where..., and..., and..., because..., however..., but ...

End with a decision.

So .... !

Now .... !

REDRAFTING AND IMPROVING

Work with another student. Read each other's soliloquies and make improvements by:

- adding extra clauses to show extra thoughts
- adding words and phrases that deepen the mood you wish to create
- using language that suggests actions for the actor

Check your soliloquy to ensure:

- it can be spoken dramatically on stage
- it begins by stating the problem the character faces
- it reaches a decision at the end

6 Looking back

- A Shakespeare **soliloquy** explores many different aspects of a problem facing the character. It helps the audience to understand what is going on in the character's mind.

- A combination of **long and short sentences** can help to get across the way a character is thinking.

- Shakespeare uses **emotive words** that help to create the atmosphere and have an effect on the audience's feelings.

Storytelling

1 ▷ Purpose

In this unit you will:

- read a story, told to get out of a difficult situation
- learn about language used to tell a convincing story
- write your own story to explain what you have done or not done!

2 ▷ Hotspur's story

In King Henry IV Part I, *Hotspur won a great battle and captured many prisoners.*

King Henry sent a messenger to demand that Hotspur hand the prisoners over to him. But Hotspur has not handed over the prisoners. Now, face-to-face with King Henry, Hotspur explains why he did not comply with the King's demand.

My **liege**, I did deny no prisoners.		*lord*
But I remember when the fight was done		
When I was dry with rage and extreme toil,		
Breathless and faint, leaning upon my sword		
5 Came there a certain lord, neat and trimly dressed,		
Fresh as a bridegroom, and his chin **new reaped**,		*fresh-shaved*
Showed like a **stubble-land** at harvest-home.		*newly-harvested field*
He was perfumed like a **milliner**,		*maker of women's hats*
And 'twixt his finger and his thumb he held		
10 A **pouncet-box**, which ever and anon		*small box for herbs or snuff*
He gave his nose and took't away again,		
Who therewith angry, when it next came there,		
Took it in snuff. And **still** he smiled and talked.		*sneezed; always*

And as the soldiers bore dead bodies by,
15 He called them untaught knaves, unmannerly,
To bring a slovenly unhandsome corpse
Betwixt the wind and his nobility.
With many **holiday and lady** terms   *unsoldierly and effeminate*
He questioned me. Amongst the rest demanded
20 My prisoners in your majesty's behalf.
I then, all smarting with my wounds being cold,
To be so pestered with a **popinjay**,   *noisy parrot*
Out of my grief and my impatience
Answered neglectingly, I know not what,
25 He should, or he should not, for he made me mad
To see him shine so brisk, and smell so sweet,
And talk so like a waiting-gentlewoman
Of guns, and drums, and wounds, God save the mark!
And telling me the **sovereignest** thing on earth   *most important*
30 Was **parmacity** for an inward bruise,   *whale-oil*
And that it was great pity, so it was,
This villainous **saltpetre** should be digged   *mineral used to make gunpowder*
Out of the bowels of the harmless earth,
Which many a good tall fellow had destroyed
35 So cowardly, and but for these vile guns
He would himself have been a soldier.
This **bald unjointed** chat of his, my lord,   *empty-headed and irrelevant*
I answered indirectly, as I said,
And I beseech you, let not his report
40 **Come current** for an accusation   *be held true*
Betwixt my love and your high majesty.

3 > Key features

Hotspur uses language techniques that he hopes will get him out of a tight spot:

- flattering words to describe the King
- unfavourable images to create a negative impression of the King's messenger
- a tone of impatience as he piles detail on detail
- a story with a clear beginning, middle and end

>> ● Why does Hotspur tell his story?
  ● Who does he blame for not obeying the King's order?
  ● What is Hotspur's view of the messenger?

4 ▸ Language skills

Word

Shakespeare always carefully chooses the **vocabulary** with which to tell his stories. Hotspur is a soldier, so his story is full of words about battles and war.

1 Write down all the 'military' words in Hotspur's story (words about fighting and warfare). How many can you find?

Shakespeare, like other writers, uses **emotive words** when he wants the language to have a particular effect on the audience's emotions.

Hotspur wants the King to believe his story. So he uses emotive words to address the king, to describe himself, and to describe the messenger. He makes a strong contrast between himself as a fighting soldier and the King's messenger as a weak and posturing courtier

2 Write down the ways in which Hotspur refers to the King in lines 1, 20, 37 and 41. Why do you think Hotspur speaks those words?

3 What words and phrases does Hotspur use to describe himself in lines 3–4, 21 and 23? What do they tell you about Hotspur?

4 What words and phrases does he use to describe the messenger in lines 5–8, 26–27? How do these descriptions contrast with those Hotspur uses about himself?

In line 22 Hotspur uses **alliteration**, repeated consonant sounds:

pestered with a popinjay

5 Write down some alliterative phrases of your own that Hotspur might have used to show his impatience and contempt for the messenger. To get you started, here are two:

bothered with a blubbing boy
needled by a nitwit

Sentence

Varying **sentence length** helps to make a story more effective. Using a variety of short and long sentences, Hotspur tries to persuade the angry King to see his point of view.

1 Work through Hotspur's story, a sentence at a time. Write in your own words what he says in each sentence. For example:

line 1   *I did not refuse to give up my prisoners*

lines 2–7   *But after the battle, I was exhausted, and...*

Hotspur uses **similes** to make his story more interesting. Similes are comparisons using like or as, for example:

Fresh as a bridegroom

2 Write down some similes of your own to describe the messenger:

line 6   fresh as _____
line 8   perfumed like _____
line 27 talk so like a _____

Hotspur also uses **metaphors** to make his story more vivid and persuasive. Metaphors are comparisons that do not use *like* or *as*, for example:

his chin new reaped means
he was freshly shaved.

Hotspur detests the way the messenger talked. He dismisses it as *holiday and lady terms* and *bald unjointed chat*.

3 Invent other metaphors which Hotspur might have used to express his contempt for the messenger's style of talking. To get you started:

*budgerigar burbling
unsorted jigsaw jabbering*

Text

Hotspur wants to persuade the King to see his **point of view**. The King wants to know why Hotspur has not obeyed his royal command to deliver the prisoners. Hotspur's story is a solution to this 'get out of that!' situation.

1 At the end of many stories that make excuses, the purpose of telling the story is revealed. What does the end of Hotspur's story show his purpose to be?

Hotspur is a soldier who values bravery, and he is contemptuous of those who do not fight. His tale of what the messenger said is in **reported speech**, telling what the messenger said. Hotspur probably mimics the messenger's language in the description of the soldiers (*untaught knaves, unmannerly, slovenly unhandsome corpse*) and in lines 29–36.

2 Speak lines 29–36 as Hotspur probably speaks them.

3 Now imagine you are the messenger. Write out lines 29–36 as direct speech, that is, as the messenger spoke them. You might begin: 'I think the best thing…'

At two places in his story, Hotspur uses **evasive language**. This is a style of speaking that avoids answering a question or does not say clearly what happened.

4 Find the lines in which Hotspur avoids saying directly what he actually said to the king's messenger when he was asked to give up his prisoners.

5 What do you think Hotspur actually said to the messenger? Imagine you are Hotspur and write down the reply he probably gave.

5 ▷ Planning your own writing

A convincing story contains detailed and lively descriptions of characters and their actions. For example in lines 3–4 Hotspur gives at least six descriptions of himself after the battle. He goes on to pile detail upon detail to build up a negative portrait of the messenger. The structure of Hotspur's story is:

- the situation
  (after a battle)
- how I felt
  (exhausted!)
- what the messenger looked like
  (unsoldierly)
- what he did
  (behaved disdainfully)
- what he said
  (contemptible nonsense!)
- how I reacted
  (can't really remember!)

Use the structure of Hotspur's story to write your own story to justify not doing what you have been told to do.

▷▷ STARTING POINT

First, invent your character and what they have been asked to do. Here are some examples for you to choose from:

- a pop musician who has not paid his or her income tax
- a famous sportsman or woman who did not turn up for an important match
- a supermodel who refused to parade on the cat-walk
- a pupil who has not done his or her homework (not you of course!)

Next, invent the person to whom you are telling your story. This could be, for example, the income tax inspector, the team manager, the fashion show organiser and a head teacher.

Finally, invent the 'messenger' you are going to blame for not doing what you were asked.

▷▷ CLUES FOR SUCCESS

- Make the person to whom you are telling the story feel important and respected.
- Write in the style of the character you have chosen.
- Remember, your excuse is that the 'messenger', not you, is to blame! So, like Hotspur, give detailed but exaggerated descriptions of:

  what they looked like
  what they did
  what they said

WRITING FRAME

Some paragraphs of your story might begin as follows:

> I had just finished...
> I was feeling...
> Suddenly,...
> He/she was dressed in...
> He/she... (what they did)
> He/she said...
> I...
> So please...

REDRAFTING AND IMPROVING

In groups or with another student, read your own and other students' first drafts. Make suggestions for improving, editing or adding more detail. Use the suggestions to redraft and improve your own version:

- Does the storyteller's personality shine through clearly?

- Have you used an appropriate and imaginative vocabulary?

- Do you mimic the 'messenger' in an exaggerated but effective style?

- Is your story convincing?

- Is the language appropriate to your chosen character who is telling the story?

- Does your story reveal that you are trying to excuse yourself by blaming someone else?

6 ▶ Looking back

- Shakespeare chooses **vocabulary** to suit the speaker and the story.

- A variety of different **sentence lengths**, and an imaginative use of **similes** and **metaphors**, can make a story more interesting to listen to.

- A **persuasive speech** has a particular point of view.

Insults

O viper vile!

1 **Purpose**

In this unit you will:
- read examples of Shakespeare's insults
- learn about the language of insults
- make up your own insults

2 **Enjoy the insults!**

Here are just a few of Shakespeare's insults

Away, you mouldy rogue, away!

Thou cream-faced loon!

26

Toads, beetles, bats, light on you!

Base, proud, shallow, beggarly, three-suited, hundred-pound, filthy worsted-stocking knave.

Thou clay-brained guts! Thou knotty-pated fool!

3 Key features

Shakespeare's insults
- use unusual words
- link words together with a hyphen
- often make up a long list
- are intended to entertain the audience

»
- Which insult do you like most? Why?
- Which insult do you like least? Why?
- Which insult does not describe someone?

27

4 ▷ Language skills

Word

Insults use a mixture of **familiar words** (like *fool*) and **unusual words** (like *worsted-stocking*)

1 Which words in each insult are new to you? Can you guess their meaning? If you are not sure, try looking them up in a dictionary.

Shakespeare enjoyed creating new expressions by joining words together with a **hyphen**: a punctuation mark (-) as in *cream-faced*. This new expression is called a **hyphenated word**.

2 Identify all the insulting words made with a hyphen. What picture comes into your mind for each of these hyphenated words?

3 Write down some hyphenated words of your own. Begin by using some of Shakespeare's expressions as your model:

_____ -brained
_____ -pated (or in modern English: _____ -headed)

A Shakespearean insult often contains an **adjective**: a word added to a noun to describe it. Adjectives give extra force to insults, because they add a rude or offensive description: *mouldy* in *mouldy rogue*.

4 What picture does 'mouldy' conjure up in your mind? Write some adjectives that describe what you 'see'.

5 Which insult does not contain an adjective?

Insults nearly always contain a **noun**, a word which labels a person, thing, feeling or idea:

viper or *knave*

6 Use a dictionary or a thesaurus to find alternative nouns and adjectives you could use in the insults. Rewrite each insult. For example, *O viper vile* might become *O snake unsavoury, O serpent sordid, O reptile repellent.*

Sentence

Two insults are **imperatives**, giving an order to somebody or something to do something. They use verbs: words which name an action.

1 Find the two imperatives, and write down the verb in each.

2 Write the other four insults as imperatives. To help you, Shakespeare was very fond of the verb *Avaunt!* meaning *Clear off!* as in *Avaunt, and quit my sight!* So the first could be A*vaunt, thou viper vile*!

Some of the insults contain **alliteration**: the repetition of consonant sounds. Alliteration helps the speaker to add force to the insult as they say it:

O Viper vile!

3 Try changing some of the words in each insult to create alliteration and add to the effect:

Bugs, beetles, bats, bombard you!

The **word order** of a sentence is important. Putting words in an appropriate order helps to convey meaning and add to the effect. In insults, adjectives are usually placed before nouns.

4 Rewrite the word order of each insult to find if it changes the force with which the insult can be spoken.

Shakespeare often piles up words to make a long **list**. The actor can speak each item in the list in a different way.

5 Write out each insult, but add extra words to create a list that will amuse the audience.

Text

Shakespeare wrote all his insults as **dramatic language**, to be spoken on stage. They are different from real life insults which are intended to hurt. In contrast, Shakespeare's insults were written to entertain the audience. So he used **colourful and imaginative language** to make up his insults.

In order to surprise his audience and make them laugh, Shakespeare looked for unusual ways of creating the insults his characters speak.

So instead of calling someone *dim* or *stupid*, he invented *clay-brained* and *knotty-pated*. The audience would laugh at the image of someone whose head (*pate* was an old word for *head*) was made of clay or full of knots.

1 A Shakespearean insult is always spoken by one character on stage. Because Falstaff is a fat character Prince Hal calls him *guts*. In reply Falstaff calls the Prince *you tailor's-yard*, meaning a ruler that tailors used for measuring cloth. What does this tell you about Prince Hal's physical appearance?

2 Think about each insult. Write down or draw your guess for each insult and guess what the character who is being insulted is like.

Because Shakespeare wrote 400 years ago, he used the **language of the time**. His audience would find *worsted-stocking* (woollen stocking) funny, because the insult is spoken to someone who thinks a lot of himself, but woollen stockings were worn only by poor people.

3 Write down one, two or three words from each insult that you think are good examples of the language of Shakespeare's time.

5 ▷ Planning your own writing

You are now writing a play. Create two characters who insult each other. Remember, your play will be seen by an audience, and you must entertain them, not offend them! Make your insults original – avoid modern-day swear words or other offensive expressions which are already in use.

Two of Shakespeare's ideas can help you:

1 Here are just a few examples of how Shakespeare used the hyphen to create insults:

> *lack-brained* *marble-hearted*
> *hard-hearted* *long-tongued*
>
> *iron-witted* *foul-spoken*
> *stretch-mouthed*

Say what you think each hyphenated word suggests the insulted character is like. Make up your own insults using the hyphen.

2 *Knave* was an old word for villain or someone who was cunning and deceitful. Here are just a few of the insults that Shakespeare created by adding adjectives to *knave*:

> *rascally, yeaforsooth knave*
>
> *poor, decayed, ingenious, foolish, rascally knave*
>
> *slipper and subtle knave*
>
> *lily-livered, action-taking knave*

Look up *knave* in a thesaurus and find other nouns to use in its place to make your own insults.

▷▷ STARTING POINTS

- Two politicians insult each other.
- Two Elizabethan actors insult each other's acting ability.
- Two snobbish people try to get the better of each other.
- Two pop singers insult each other's talent.

▷▷ CLUES FOR SUCCESS

- Use a thesaurus to find unusual words.
- Invent new words using the hyphen.
- Turn some insults into imperatives.
- Pile up adjectives into long lists that end with a noun.

▷▷ REDRAFTING AND IMPROVING

Work with another student. Read each other's insults. Make improvements by:

- thinking up more unusual words
- changing the order of words in the insult
- correcting spelling mistakes
- adding words to make a longer list

Now write your final versions of your insults. Use a word processor and explore how different styles of presentation can make your insults more powerful.

WRITING FRAMES

1 Make up your own insult generator!
Copy out the following and add your own adjectives and nouns

adjective	adjective	noun
meddling	lily-livered	shrimp
juggling	puppy-headed	tickle-brain
....	....	....
....	....	....

2 Or create an imperative insult generator!

verb	adjective	noun
Go	revolting	bubble
Avaunt	lack-linen	waterfly
____	____	____
____	____	____

Generators work by choosing one word from each column to form an insult:

Avaunt, you lack-linen bubble!

6 > Looking back

Check through your **insults** and make sure that:
- each one would entertain an audience
- your insults are fresh and unusual
- you have created new words with the **hyphen**

Imagery

In this unit you will:

- read examples of Shakespeare's use of imagery
- learn about the language of imagery
- write your own examples of imagery

2 ▷ Shakespeare's imagery

King Henry V uses a powerful image to urge his soldiers on to a new attack:

Then imitate the action of the tiger

In King Henry VI Part 3, *Queen Margaret describes her three enemies:*

And what is Edward but a ruthless sea?
What Clarence but a quicksand of deceit?
What Richard but a ragged, fatal rock?

In *Macbeth*, *Angus pictures Macbeth as a man who has no right to be king*:

> Now does he feel his title
> Hang loose about him, like a giant's robe
> Upon a dwarfish thief.

In *The Merchant of Venice*, *Portia describes mercy*:

> The quality of mercy is not strained,
> It droppeth as the gentle rain from heaven

Hamlet turns death into an officer arresting a criminal (fell means cruel or deadly):

> This fell sergeant Death
> is strict in his arrest

3 ❯ Key features

Imagery

- creates vivid pictures in the imagination
- makes unexpected and unusual comparisons that appeal to the reader or audience
- uses emotionally charged words and phrases
- creates atmosphere, and gives insight into characters' feelings
- uses metaphor, simile or personification

➤➤
- Which image uses questions, and which is an order?
- Which picture helps you most with the language? Why?
- Which of the five images do you like best? Why?

4 ▶ Language skills

Word

Imagery frequently uses very familiar **nouns** as the basis of the comparison, for example, in Queen Margaret's image: *sea, quicksand, rock*

❶ What familiar nouns are used in the other imagery examples?

Sometimes an image is made up of two nouns: *quicksand of deceit* (a quicksand is a dangerous area of beach like a swamp or bog)

❷ Which other images use two nouns?

The nouns are usually accompanied by one or more **adjectives** that give a special meaning to the phrase:

And what is Edward but a ruthless sea (the adjective *ruthless* means pitiless)

What Richard but a ragged, fatal rock (the adjectives *ragged, fatal* mean jagged, deadly)

❸ What other **adjective** + **noun** phrases can you find in the imagery examples? Write them down.

❹ Add adjectives to the following nouns to create images of your own that convey the same general meaning as those in the examples, The first is done for you.

   merciless   sea
_____ rock
_____ thief
_____ rain
_____ sergeant

Sentence

Shakespeare builds up imagery using carefully chosen **vocabulary**, **simile**, **metaphor** and **personification**. The language of each image calls up an unusual and vivid picture in your mind, like imagining a soldier as a fearless tiger.

A **simile** is a way of comparing things in an unusual or unexpected way, in which the writer uses the words **like** or **as**:

> *like a giant's robe*
> *as the gentle rain*

A **metaphor** is also a way of comparing two things, but without using **like or as**. A metaphor seems to say that something is really something else:

> Edward = *a ruthless sea*
> Clarence = *a quicksand of deceit*

A **personification** is a special kind of metaphor. It turns all kinds of things (objects, ideas, feelings) into persons, and names them with a capital letter:

> *This fell sergeant Death*

If you changed Henry V's image into a metaphor, it could be:

> *Become tigers in your actions!*

If you changed it to a simile, it could be:

> *Be like a tiger in your actions!* or
> *Be as fierce as a tiger!*

1 Now work through the other imagery examples changing metaphors into similes, and similes into metaphors. Write down your answers like this:

And what is Edward but a ruthless sea? = metaphor

And is not Edward like a ruthless sea? = simile

2 Say whether the following are metaphors or similes, then change the metaphors to similes, and the similes to metaphors. The first one is done for you to show you how to write your answer:

Life's but a walking shadow
        = metaphor.

Life is only like a walking shadow
        = simile

Life's but a walking shadow

The whining schoolboy creeping like snail unwillingly to school

There's daggers in men's smiles

I am as melancholy as a gib cat
        (howling tomcat)

The moon, like to a silver bow new bent in heaven

Now is the winter of our discontent

Look like the innocent flower, but be the serpent under it
(two types of imagery here!)

I can swim like a duck

Text

Imagery (which is sometimes called **figurative language**) adds to the effect of a text by helping to create atmosphere or character.

1 Look at the images on pages 32–33 and for each one write down:

- what atmosphere or mood it seems to create

- what it might reveal about the speaker's personality (the kind of person who would use such an image)

- what you think the speaker is trying to achieve by using the image

2 How easy do you find it to conjure up pictures in your mind when you read an image on pages 32–33? Try drawing some of the pictures you think of when you read the images. Which images do you find easiest to imagine and to draw? Why?

3 Talk together with another student about the images in this unit and compare your 'mental pictures'. How different are they? After your discussion, write down the images which appeal to you most, and give one or two reasons why you enjoy them.

35

5 ▷ Planning your own writing

1 Collect examples of imagery from newspapers and magazines (imagery is often used in headlines). Identify what kind of images they are (metaphors, similes or personification), and say whether you think they are effective.

2 Television and radio programmes of all kinds use imagery frequently. For example, in a popular series, one character said she was 'head over heels' in love. That's a metaphor. What picture does it conjure up in your mind? Write down examples as you hear them.

3 Build up your own 'data bank' (that's an image!) of images. Use it to create your own effective images in your writing.

4 One of the best ways of learning to write imagery is to use Shakespeare as a model. Take any of the examples in this unit and write your own images instead of Shakespeare's.

▷▷ STARTING POINTS

Here are some well known images that have become clichés (over-used, over-familiar). Say what kind of image each one is (metaphor or simile). Then freshen them up by rewriting each to create a new and vivid image:

- The goalkeeper was as sick as a parrot.
- The goalscorer was over the moon.
- The man is a snake in the grass.
- It was raining cats and dogs.
- The athlete ran like lightning.
- The woman is a pain in the neck.
- The toddler is as happy as a lark.
- The soldier was lion-hearted (use the hyphen to create your own image).
- The boxer floats like a butterfly, and stings like a bee.

▷▷ CLUES FOR SUCCESS

- Begin with a familiar noun.
- Add one or more adjectives to make an unexpected but appropriate image.
- Think whether metaphor or simile or personification might be more effective.
- Think of comparisons using animals or birds, the seasons, the sea, sun, moon and stars — or anything that you feel is appropriate.

WRITING FRAMES

Imagery for a person:
He/she looked like ....
His eyes .... and his .... mouth ....
He moved as if ....
He/she was ....
(Now carry on using imagery to describe what he/she did.)

Imagery for a place or time:
The sun rose like ....
All the trees ....
The fields were ....
The farmer .... as a ....
It was a .... day
(Now carry on using imagery to describe what happened.)

REDRAFTING AND IMPROVING

Work with another student. Read each other's examples of imagery. Can you make improvements by:

- using more effective nouns and adjectives?
- changing similes to metaphors?
- extending the image with additional comparisons?

6 Looking back

- **Imagery** uses lively and imaginative language.
- Imagery can be expressed as **metaphor**, **simile** or **personification**.
- The language of imagery often links people and things together in unusual but memorable ways, suggesting they are the same as, or like each other.

Comedy and repetition

1 ▶ Purpose

In this unit you will:

- read an example of how Shakespeare uses repetition
- learn about different kinds of repetition in language
- write a dramatic scene of your own using repetition

2 ▶ The death of Pyramus and Thisbe

At the end of A Midsummer Night's Dream, *the mechanicals (workmen) present their play about the two lovers Pyramus and Thisbe. Bottom the weaver plays Pyramus, and Flute the bellows-mender plays Thisbe.*

Thisbe has been frightened away by a Lion played by Snug the joiner. Thisbe leaves her cloak behind which the Lion savages. Pyramus enters and sees the cloak...

PYRAMUS	Sweet Moon, I thank thee for thy sunny beams;
	I thank thee Moon, for shining now so bright;
	For by thy gracious, golden, glittering gleams,
	I trust to take of truest Thisbe sight.
5	But stay! O spite!
	But mark, Poor Knight,
	What dreadful **dole** is here!
	Eyes, do you see?
	How can it be?
10	O dainty duck! O dear!
	Thy **mantle** good,
	What, stained with blood?
	Approach, ye **Furies** fell!
	O **Fates**, come, come,
15	Cut **thread** and **thrum**,
	Quail, crush, **conclude**, and quell!

Glosses (right margin):
- *sadness* (for **dole**)
- *cloak* (for **mantle**)
- *cruel avenging goddesses* (for **Furies**)
- *goddesses who wove and cut the threads of each human life* (for **Fates**)
- *destroy* (for **conclude**)

	Come, tears, **confound**!	*prevent*
	Out sword, and wound	
	The **pap** of Pyramus.	*breast*
20	Ay, that left pap,	
	Where heart doth hop. *[Stabs himself]*	
	Thus die I, thus, thus, thus!	
	Now am I dead,	
	Now am I fled;	
25	My soul is in the sky.	
	Tongue, lose thy light,	
	Moon, take thy flight;	
	Now die, die, die, die, die! *[Dies]*	
	[Enter Thisbe]	

THISBE	Asleep, my love?	
30	What, dead, my dove?	
	O Pyramus, arise!	
	Speak, speak! Quite dumb?	
	Dead, dead? A tomb	
	Must cover thy sweet eyes.	
35	These lily lips,	
	This cherry nose,	
	These yellow cowslip cheeks,	
	Are gone, are gone!	
	Lovers make moan;	
40	His eyes were green as leeks.	
	O **Sisters Three**,	*goddesses of fate*
	Come, come to me,	
	With hands as pale as milk;	
	Lay them in **gore**,	*blood*
48	Since you have **shore**	*cut*
	With shears his thread of silk.	
	Tongue, not word!	
	Come, trusty sword,	
	Come, blade, my breast **imbrue**!	*make bloody*
50	And farewell, friends.	
	Thus Thisbe ends!	
	Adieu, adieu, adieu! *[Dies]*	

3 Key features

Shakespeare uses:
- repeated words and phrases
- repeated sounds, rhymes and rhythms
- repeated actions and events

➤
- At what line does Bottom's mood change?
- Which line do you like most? Why?
- How do you think the audience responds to this scene?

4 Language skills

Word

The **vocabulary** of the scene, the words used in the text, is full of repetitions, especially of **key words** that help to create the scene's special atmosphere.

1 Which key words are repeated in the text? Write notes which advise the actors how to speak these repeated words in ways that will make the audience laugh.

The scene contains many examples of **alliteration**, the repetition of consonants, usually at the beginning of words:

thy gracious, golden, glittering gleams

2 How many examples of alliteration can you find in the text? In pairs, decide which one appeals to you most and explain why you like it.

Rhyme is the repetition of words which make the same sounds, usually at the end of a line.

The **rhyme scheme** is the pattern of rhymes in the text: which lines rhyme with which. For example, line 1 rhymes with line 3; line 2 rhymes with line 4.

3 Speak aloud just the words at the end of each line to find which lines rhyme with which. Try to write down the rhyme scheme of both speeches. Are they similar?

Some lines may not seem to rhyme. That is because **pronunciation** has changed since Shakespeare's time. For example, in his day *word* and *sword* could sound the same and so rhyme.

4 Write down the words in the text which rhymed in Shakespeare's time, but do not rhyme today. Make a guess at how those words might have been pronounced in Shakespeare's day.

Sentence

Actors use **punctuation** as a guide to speaking, because it helps them decide how long a pause is needed between different parts of a sentence.

comma (,) a slight pause

semicolon (;) a slightly longer pause

full stop (.) the end of a sentence, a longer pause.

exclamation mark (!) tells the speaker to add extra emphasis to the word or phrase

1 Work with another student and speak the lines using the punctuation as a guide to where to pause and add emphasis.

Find lines where you could use different punctuation to increase the audience's enjoyment of the scene.

In drama, when a character speaks, what he or she says is called a **speech**. The pattern of Thisbe's speech contains echoes or mirror images of Pyramus' speech. The two speeches repeat each other in **rhythms**, **actions** and **thoughts**. Both Pyramus and Thisbe have 24 lines each in the same style:

Pyramus	*lines 5–28*
Thisbe	*lines 29–52*

2 To find how these lines mirror and repeat each other, speak a line from one speech, followed by a line from the other. For example, speak line 5, then line 29. Then speak line 6 followed by line 30, and so on to the end of both speeches. Make an action as you speak each line. When you have finished, write down the ways in which the two speeches repeat each other.

Text

Shakespeare wrote the Pyramus and Thisbe play as a **parody**: a mocking imitation of a style of writing. It makes fun of **tragedies** of love like *Romeo and Juliet*. But it also pokes fun at the **repetition** techniques in language that Shakespeare had learned about at school.

Shakespeare intended the audience to laugh at all the repetitions. So actors use all kinds of methods to increase audience amusement.

1 Imagine you are directing Pyramus and Thisbe. Write notes to help the actors on each of the following points:

- Should the actors attempt to rhyme all through, even though some words do not rhyme today?

- How could Pyramus speak each *die* in a different way to make the audience laugh at each?

- How could you use the repetitions to make the 'deaths' of Pyramus and Thisbe at lines 28 and 52 as funny as possible?

- Should Bottom and Flute speak their lines very seriously all through?

Stage directions tell the actors what to do. They are given in italics in brackets *[Dies]*.

2 Work through the text, inventing more stage directions to help the actors make the audience laugh even more.

Actors always have a choice of whether they speak to **another character**, to **themselves**, or to the **audience**.

3 Write down the line numbers of the lines you think the actors could speak directly to the audience to increase the humour of the scene.

5 ▷ Planning your own writing

- Listen to people talking. How often do they use repetitions as they speak?

- Look through magazines and newspapers. What examples of repetition can you find?

- Think of examples from television and radio. What characters have catch phrases they repeat? What other repetitions are used?

- To help your own writing just copy Shakespeare!

- Write a parody: a 'send up' or mocking imitation of a style of writing. It can be a scene of a play that deliberately makes fun of different ways of repeating language: words, sounds, rhymes, rhythms.

After you have written your parody, you could write something more serious using the techniques of repetition you have learned.

▷▷ STARTING POINTS

- A parody of an episode of a television series.

- A parody of a historical event:
  Julius Caesar invading Britain
  William the Conqueror at the Battle of Hastings
  A landing on the moon

- A teacher asks for a pupil's homework (the pupil has not done it!)

- A parody of a scene from a Shakespeare play (Romeo speaks to Juliet?)

▷▷ CLUES FOR SUCCESS

- Repeat words and phrases.

- Use repeated exclamations.

- Use strong rhythms and clear rhymes.

- Make the ending funny and absurd.

⟫ WRITING FRAME

Use Shakespeare's rhyme scheme with your own words:

.... dead,
.... fled;
.... sky.
.... light,
.... flight;
.... die!

⟫ REDRAFTING AND IMPROVING

Work with another student.
Read each other's scenes and see how you
could make any improvements.

- Repeat other words.
- Add extra rhymes.
- Add more alliteration.
- Write lines that can be accompanied with
  repeated actions.

Now write your final version, take parts and act it out!

Check through your scene.

- Have you included alliteration and rhyme?
- Do the different speakers mirror each other
  in some way?
- Can the actors repeat the same actions for
  different lines?

Now try writing a serious scene using repetitions.

6 ⟩ Looking back

- **Repetition** of words
  can help to create
  the scene's special
  atmosphere.

- Actors use
  punctuation to
  guide them in how
  to say the lines.

- A **parody** is a
  mocking imitation.

- Shakespeare wrote
  Pyramus and
  Thisbe as a parody
  of tragedies and of
  well-known repetitive
  styles of poetry.

Dramatic openings

1 ▶ **Purpose**

In this unit you will:
- read the opening scene of *Macbeth*
- learn how Shakespeare wrote dramatic openings to his plays
- write your own opening scene of a play

2 ▶ **Amaze the audience**

In *Macbeth* Act I Scene 1 the witches meet in a desolate place.

	[Thunder and lightning. Enter three witches]	
	FIRST WITCH	When shall we three meet again?	
		In thunder, lightning, or in rain?	
	SECOND WITCH	When the hurly-burly's done,	
		When the battle's lost and won.	
5	THIRD WITCH	That will be **ere** the set of sun.	*before*
	FIRST WITCH	Where the place?	
	SECOND WITCH	Upon the heath.	
	THIRD WITCH	There to meet with Macbeth.	
	FIRST WITCH	I come, Graymalkin.	
10	SECOND WITCH	Paddock calls.	
	THIRD WITCH	**Anon**	*At once!*
	ALL WITCHES	Fair is foul, and foul is fair,	
		Hover through the fog and filthy air.	
	[Exeunt]	

3 > Key features

An opening scene seizes the audience's interest with:

- a stage direction that gives opportunities for dramatic acting and settings
- a gripping first line
- a forecast of conflict to come
- an intense atmosphere created with emotive words and phrases

>>
- What do you think the witches look like?
- Where are they? What kind of place is it?
- What do they do as they speak?

45

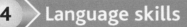

Dramatic openings

4 ▶ Language skills

Word

An opening scene uses an **appropriate vocabulary**: a choice of words to create a particular atmosphere or mood.

❶ Write down a sentence describing the atmosphere of the scene. Which words help to create that atmosphere?

The word *hurly-burly* sounds like what it is: a noisy, excited commotion, like a fight. It is an example of **onomatopoeia**: words whose sound echoes their meaning.

Other examples of onomatopoeia are words like *splash*, *jingle*, *thump*, *crash* and *slap*.

❷ Write down the word onomatopoeia (everybody finds it difficult to spell!) and list as many words as you can think of whose sound echoes their meaning.

Graymalkin and Paddock are **proper nouns**, the names of a cat and a toad. These two creatures are the witches' familiars – animals which help witches with their magic. But in the play the witches' own names are never revealed.

❸ What do you think are appropriate names for the witches? Invent three proper nouns.

Sentence

Shakespeare's language creates a dramatic opening to the play. He uses **questions** to produce a feeling of mystery and suspense.

❶ Explore ways of speaking the questions to make them sound mysterious and strange

Shakespeare uses **short sentences** to build up a sense of urgency and threat.

❷ Do you think the short sentences should be spoken quickly or slowly? Experiment with different speeds of speaking the scene. Write notes about the pace at which you think each line should be spoken.

Line 12 is an example of a **palindromic sentence**. These are words that are the same whether you read them left to right or right to left. It is rather like a **palindrome**: a phrase which reads the same forwards or backwards, for example *Madam I'm Adam*.

❸ Read line 12 in both directions, forwards and backwards. Does it sound like a witches' spell? Now write down some sentences of your own that read the same in both directions

Text

All plays have **stage directions**: instructions to the actors what to do; sound effects and other ways of creating atmosphere. The first stage direction of any play is an invitation to the imagination of the actors and director: how can they create a thrilling dramatic opening?

The simple word *Enter* does not mean that the actors walk on stage. They appear in a way that the audience will find dramatic and interesting.

1 Make notes on how you would stage the opening stage direction to achieve the greatest dramatic effect.

The final **stage direction is** *Exeunt*. This a **technical word**: a word which is used only in a particular context. *Exeunt* is Latin for 'Everybody leaves the stage'.

2 *Exeunt* is a **plural** technical word used only in plays. The **singular** of *Exeunt* is in everyday use today, and you see it as a sign in many places. What is it? A clue: it begins with the same two letters.

The scene ends with a **rhyming couplet**: two lines that rhyme. Shakespeare ends many of his scenes with a couplet. It was a reminder to the audience that the scene was ending, and a kind of summary of what had happened or what was to come.

3 Write a couplet of your own that could end the scene in a mysterious way. Make sure that you keep to a four-beat rhythm like the witches' couplet.

An opening scene introduces one or more of the major **themes** of the play. A theme is an idea or issue that the play is about. It runs all through the play.

4 One theme of *Macbeth* is conflict. Find some words or phrases in the language that seem to be about conflict and trouble, now or in the future.

Shakespeare provides the witches with **appropriate language** which is mysterious and spell-like. It has **rhythm** and **rhyme** which create an eerie atmosphere of witchcraft and magic.

5 How many rhymes can you find? Write them down. With another student, discuss whether the witches should emphasise the rhymes as they speak. Give reasons for your decision.

6 Work together in a group of three and explore ways of speaking the scene to create a magical effect.

47

5 ▶ Planning your own writing

The opening scenes of Shakespeare's plays are intended to thrill the audience.

Hamlet begins with a sentry's challenge: 'Who's there?'

The Tempest opens with a terrible storm at sea and a shipwreck.

In *A Midsummer Night's Dream*, an angry father demands the death of his own daughter if she will not obey him.

Write the opening scene of your own play. Electrify your audience!

▶▶ STARTING POINTS

Decide what your play is about, and several of the characters in it:

- A spaceship crew receives an frightening message.
- Witches plan to visit your school.
- A sentry hears a noise in the darkness.
- A king is challenged by one of his courtiers.

▶▶ CLUES FOR SUCCESS

- Have only two or three speaking characters.
- Begin with a question.
- Use short sentences.
- Use a vocabulary full of words that echo the theme of your play.
- Create conflict: now or to come!

➤➤ WRITING FRAMES

Opening stage direction: Where does the scene take place?

Who enters?

Opening line: Is it exciting?

Conflict: Do the characters clash?

Final two lines: Write a couplet.

Final stage direction: Exeunt (but how?)

➤➤ REDRAFTING AND IMPROVING

Work with another student and read each other's opening scene.

- Can you make any improvements by changing the stage directions?
- Will adding words and phrases increase dramatic effect?
- Can you invent a more powerful ending?

Check through your scene.

- Is the opening line thrilling?
- Does the scene contain conflict?
- Does it end in a very dramatic way?
- Will it appeal to the imagination of your audience?
- Is there a sense of mystery and urgency?

6 ▷ Looking back

- **Questions** can help to create a feeling of mystery and suspense in the opening moments.
- **Short sentences** build up a sense of urgency and threat.
- **Stage directions** are important because they tell the actors what to do or give instructions about sound and lighting effects.

Now write the final version of your scene. Word process it and print out copies.

Work in a group and act out your scene.

Lists

Purpose

In this unit you will:
- read one of Shakespeare's lists
- learn how lists can interest readers and create dramatic effect
- write your own lists to entertain readers and to be acted out dramatically

2 **The seven ages of man**

In As You Like It, *Jaques imagines the world as a stage, with all human beings as actors. He describes the seven ages of man.*

All the world's a stage,
And all the men and women merely **players**.   *actors*
They have their exits and their entrances,
And one man in his time plays many parts,
His Acts being seven ages. At first the infant,
Mewling and **puking** in the nurse's arms.   *crying and vomiting*
Then, the whining schoolboy, with his satchel
And shining morning face, creeping like snail
Unwillingly to school. And then the lover,
Sighing like furnace, with a woeful ballad
Made to his mistress' eyebrow. Then, a soldier,
Full of strange oaths, and bearded like the **pard**,   *leopard*
Jealous in honour, sudden and quick to quarrel,
Seeking the **bubble reputation**   *short-lived honour*
Even in the cannon's mouth. And then, the **justice**,   *judge*
In fair round belly, with good **capon** lined,   *chicken*
With eyes severe, and beard of formal cut,
Full of wise **saws** and **modern instances**,   *sayings and boring examples*

5

10

15

And so he plays his part. The sixth age shifts

20   Into the lean and slippered **pantaloon**,   *old fool in Italian comedy*

With spectacles on nose and pouch on side,

His youthful **hose**, well saved, a world too wide   *stockings breeches*

For his shrunk **shank**, and his big manly voice,   *leg*

Turning again toward childish treble, pipes

25   And whistles in his sound. Last scene of all,

That ends this strange eventful history,

Is second childishness, and mere oblivion,

Sans teeth, **sans** eyes, **sans** taste, **sans** everything.   *without*

3 Key features

In Shakespeare's lists:

- each separate item can be clearly identified
- each item is described using imaginative nouns, adjectives and verbs
- the items build up to create a total effect

>>
- Can you find a different word to describe each age? (The first could be infant or baby.)
- Which age has the shortest description?
- Which age do you find the hardest to picture in your mind? Why?

51

4 ▷ Language skills

Word

Nouns, adjectives and verbs add great liveliness to the pictures of each age of a man's life.

Nouns are words that name things, people or feelings: *stage, infant, jealousy*

❶ In the 'seven ages of man' speech the first 'age' is *infant*. Find the six nouns that describe each of the following six ages (this may not be easy for the last age!)

Adjectives are words which describe somebody or something. They help to give more information about a noun: *whining, strange, lean* and *slippered*.

❷ Which age contains no adjectives? (A clue: in this age, the verbs tell you what the age is like.)

❸ Which adjectives in the whole description do you most enjoy? Write down why you like them.

❹ Describe each age using only an adjective followed by a noun, for example a *crying baby*, *a reluctant schoolboy*. Write your list down and compare it with other students' lists.

Verbs are words that tell you what people (or things) are doing or being: *plays, puking, creeping*.

❺ Which age contains no verb to tell you what the person described is actually doing? Which verb in the 'seven ages' do you find most appealing? Write a sentence saying why you like it.

Unfamiliar words: In line 12, *pard* is an old word for leopard.

❻ What other unfamiliar words can you find? Look up their meanings in a dictionary to discover if they are the same as those given alongside the speech. Write down the dictionary definitions.

Foreign words: in the last line, the French word *sans* (meaning 'without') is used four times in the last line.

❼ Write down an English word (of only one syllable) that you could use instead of *sans* to convey the same meaning to the audience.

King Richard III grows up – see page 53.

52

Sentence

Imagery is the use of language to create striking pictures. The first sentence of the speech is a famous image, comparing human life to a stage play, with men and women as actors, playing out their lives in seven Acts (an Act is a section of a play). The rest of the speech then lists the seven ages of man. It uses:

similes – comparisons using *like* or *as*, for example *creeping like snail*

and

metaphors – comparisons that do not use *like* or *as*, for example *shining morning face*

1 Pick out the three similes in the speech. Select your favourite and write why you think it is effective.

2 Draw the picture that the following metaphors conjure up in your mind:

> *shining morning face*
> *bubble reputation*
> *with good capon lined*

3 Without getting out of your seat, read the speech a sentence at a time and accompany each line with suitable actions, gestures or expressions.

Text

There are many kinds of **lists**. A shopping list is usually a simple list of nouns: *apples, tea, sugar, potatoes* etc. Its purpose is just to be useful.

But lists in a play have different purposes. They are meant to **entertain the audience**, and to do other things, like helping to **create character or place or atmosphere**. For example, in *Macbeth* the long list of ingredients of the witches' cauldron is probably meant to chill the blood of the audience and to create a mood of evil and dangerous magic.

1 Write notes to describe how you would stage the seven ages of man so that audiences would greatly enjoy your show.

Shakespeare often writes different lists on the same **topic**. In *Richard III*, Richard's mother lists how her son developed. It is a variation of 'the seven ages of man' list:

> *Techy and wayward was thy infancy;*
> *Thy schooldays frightful, desperate,*
> *wild and furious;*
> *Thy prime of manhood, daring,*
> *bold and venturous.*
> *Thy age confirmed, proud, subtle,*
> *sly and bloody*

2 How many 'ages' are in this list? What nouns describe each 'age'?

3 Invent an action or expression to portray each adjective in the list.

4 Compare how babies, schoolboys, soldiers and mature men (*age confirmed* and *justice*) are described in this speech and in the 'seven ages' speech.

5 ▷ Planning your own writing

It is easy to compile a list. For example, you could simply write down the names of your friends, or your favourite singers or sports personalities. But try writing a list for an actor to speak on stage in ways that will entertain and fascinate audiences.

▶ STARTING POINTS

- Rewrite the 'seven ages of man' speech as 'the seven ages of woman', or the 'seven ages of a school student'.

- Write a list that describes yourself or another person.

- Write a list that describes where you live or your school.

- Rewrite the description of Richard III as Richard himself might write it. Remember that he probably has a much more positive view of himself!

▶ CLUES FOR SUCCESS

- Begin with an exciting sentence that introduces your list.

- Use lively adjectives and nouns to create imaginative imagery.

- Use one of the lists in this unit as a model for your writing.

- Check that an actor can accompany each item with an action of some sort.

▶ WRITING FRAMES

1 Use similes and metaphors

- similes: he is as brave as a lion; she has a smile like the sun
  he is as .... ;
  she is like ....

- metaphors: he is lion-hearted; she has a sunny smile
  he is .... ;
  She has ....

2 Use these descriptions of Falstaff in King Henry IV Part 2:

For each item, an adjective is followed by a noun:

a moist eye, a dry hand, a yellow cheek, a white beard

a .... eye,
a .... hand,
a .... cheek,
a .... beard

or a noun is followed by an adjective:

Is not your voice broken, your wind short, your chin double, your wit single?

Is not your voice ....,
your wind ....,
your chin ....,
your wit ....?

REDRAFTING AND IMPROVING

In groups or with another student, talk together about the first drafts of the lists you have compiled. Make suggestions for improving them. Ask yourselves these questions:

● Can you make your list more effective by including additional items?

● Can you write a more interesting introduction to your list?

● If you search through a thesaurus can you come up with some alternative words?

● Can each item be acted out in some way?

6 ▷ Looking back

● **Lists** can be used for all kinds of purposes: to create atmosphere or to describe a person or a place or a sequence of events.

● Lists can be made up of **single words**, or of **phrases**, or of **whole sentences** filled with descriptive detail.

● Lists can comprise only **nouns**, or only **adjectives**, or **combinations** of all kinds of words.

Dialogue

1 ▷ **Purpose**

In this unit you will:

- read some dialogue from *Romeo and Juliet*
- learn how dialogue is written
- write your own dialogue for a scene in a play

2 ▷ **The death of Mercutio, *Romeo and Juliet***

Tybalt wants to pick a fight with Romeo, but Romeo refuses the challenge, because he has secretly married Tybalt's cousin, Juliet. Romeo's friends, Mercutio and Benvolio are on stage, and Mercutio is looking for trouble!

TYBALT	Romeo, the love I bear thee can afford	
	No better term than this: thou art a villain.	
ROMEO	Tybalt, the reason that I have to love thee	
	Doth much excuse the **appertaining** rage	*appropriate*
5	To such a greeting. Villain am I none;	
	Therefore farewell, I see thou knowest me not.	
TYBALT	Boy, this shall not excuse the injuries	
	That thou hast done me, therefore turn and draw.	
ROMEO	I do protest I never injured thee,	
10	But love thee better than thou **canst devise**,	*can imagine*
	Till thou shalt know the reason of my love.	
	And so, good **Capulet**, which name I tender	*Tybalt*
	As dearly as mine own, be satisfied.	
MERCUTIO	O calm, dishonourable, vile submission!	
15	**'Alla stoccata'** carries it away.	*'sword thrust'*
	Tybalt, you rat-catcher, will you walk?	
	[Draws his sword]	
TYBALT	What wouldst thou have with me?	
MERCUTIO	Good King of Cats, nothing but one of your nine	
	lives that I mean to make bold withal, and as	

20	you shall use me hereafter, **dry-beat** the rest	*thrash*
	of the eight. Will you pluck your sword out	
	of his **pilcher** by the ears? Make haste, lest mine be	*scabbard*
	about your ears ere it be out.	
TYBALT	I am for you *[Draws his sword]*	
ROMEO	Gentle Mercutio, put thy rapier up.	
MERCUTIO	Come, sir, your **'passado'**	*sword thrust*
	[They fight]	
ROMEO	Draw, Benvolio, beat down their weapons.	
	Gentlemen, for shame forbear this **outrage**!	*criminal behaviour*
	Tybalt, Mercutio, the Prince expressly hath	
30	Forbid this **bandying** in Verona streets.	*brawling*
	[He steps between the fighting Mercutio and Tybalt]	
	Hold Tybalt! Good Mercutio!	
	[Tybalt thrusts his sword into Mercutio under	
	Romeo's arm. Tybalt flees]	
MERCUTIO	I am hurt;	
	A plague on both your **houses**! I am **sped**.	*families; killed*
	Is he gone and hath nothing?	
BENVOLIO	What, art thou hurt?	
MERCUTIO	Ay, ay, a scratch, a scratch, marry, 'tis enough.	
	Where is my page? Go **villain**, fetch a surgeon.	*fellow*
	[Exit Page]	
ROMEO	Courage, man, the hurt cannot be much.	
MERCUTIO	No, 'tis not so deep as a well, nor so wide as a	
40	church-door, but 'tis enough, 'twill serve. Ask for	
	me tomorrow, and you shall find me a grave man.	
	I am peppered, I warrant, for this world. A plague	
	on both your houses!	

3 ▶ Key features

In written dialogue:

- each character's name appears first, followed by what they say
- characters talk to each other, listening and responding to what has just been said
- the language often suggests actions and facial expressions
- the language tells you what the character is thinking and feeling

⟫
- Which characters are spoiling for a fight? Why?
- Who wants to avoid a fight? Why?
- In what ways are Romeo, Tybalt and Mercutio himself responsible for Mercutio's death?

4 Language skills

Word

Shakespeare's characters often use **insults**: rude or offensive words that express contempt or dislike. Tybalt calls Romeo *villain*. Mercutio speaks mockingly in Italian to ridicule Tybalt: *Alla stoccata* and *passado* both mean 'sword thrust'.

1 Write down all the words used by Tybalt and Mercutio as insults.

2 Now write all the words Romeo uses which show he wants to keep the peace.

Because the English language has changed since Shakespeare's time, **old words** or unfamiliar words, like *pilcher* instead of *scabbard* have dropped out of use.

3 Make a list of all the unfamiliar old words. Write alongside each word its modern English meaning.

In dialogue, one speaker often uses a word which has just been spoken by the previous speaker. The first examples of these **repeated words** are *love* and *villain* as Romeo replies to Tybalt.

4 In each speech, identify and write down words which show the speaker is responding to a word in the preceding speech.

Sentence

Sometimes Shakespeare alters the usual **word order** of a sentence to add dramatic effect. For example, Romeo says *Villain am I none* rather than *I am no villain*. On stage, Romeo can heavily emphasise *none* to increase the strength of his rejection of Tybalt's insult.

1 Write down any examples of unusual word order you can find in this dialogue. With another student, pick three examples, say them out loud, and, in each case, explain how the unusual word order helps to get a particular meaning across.

In dialogue, one character is always speaking to another. Each sentence, therefore, often contains the other character's **name**, or the **personal pronoun** *you* (or *thee* or *thou*).

2 Work through each speech and find the name or pronoun that tells you to whom the speech is spoken. For example, in the first speech, *Romeo*, *thee* and *thou* are used, all directed at Romeo.

Text

Stage directions are instructions telling the actors what to do. They are printed in italics in brackets: *[Draws his sword]*. Because a play is written to be acted out, every sentence contains clues to what gestures and actions the character might make. In Tybalt's first speech he might point directly at Romeo when he says *Romeo* and *Thou art a villain*.

❸ What does Romeo do when he speaks *farewell* in the following speech?

❹ Work through each speech and write down at least one gesture the actor might use.

Exclamations are words, phrase or sentences expressing emotions. They often end in an **exclamation mark** (!) Because this is a very dramatic scene, it is filled with all kinds of exclamations. For example, Mercutio knows he is mortally wounded. He knows he will die because of the feud between the rival houses (families) of the Montagues and Capulets. So he exclaims *A plague on both your houses!*

❺ What other exclamations can you find in the dialogue?

Every time a character speaks, they express their **point of view**. This shows what they are feeling and thinking. Each speech can tell you something about the character's aims: what they want to achieve (their **motive**).

❶ Consider each speech and suggest what the character wants to achieve by speaking it (his motive).

The language a character uses tells you what he or she is like. Tybalt is always looking for a fight; Romeo wants to avoid **conflict**.

❷ Read what each character says. Write what their language tells you about their personality.

Actors have to decide the **pace** at which they will speak (whether it is fast or slow); the length of each **pause** they make; and the **emphasis** they will put on particular words or phrases.

❸ Imagine you are directing a production of *Romeo and Juliet.* Write notes for the actors showing:

 ● the pace at which you think each speech should be spoken

 ● where the actor might pause

 ● which words or phrases the actor might emphasise

5 ▷ Planning your own writing

All drama is based on conflict. To write dialogue, you therefore need characters who are in conflict with each other in some way. Invent two or more characters, put them in a conflict situation, and write your dialogue.

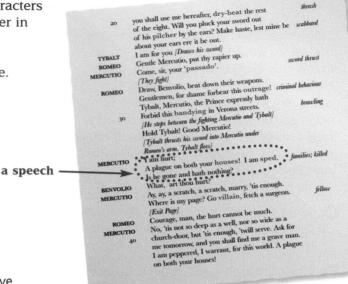

a speech →

<table>
<tr><td>20</td><td>you shall use me hereafter, dry-beat the rest of the eight. Will you pluck your sword out of his pilcher by the ears? Make haste, lest mine be about your ears ere it be out.</td><td>thrash
scabbard</td></tr>
<tr><td>TYBALT
ROMEO
MERCUTIO</td><td>I am for you [Draws his sword]
Gentle Mercutio, put thy rapier up.
Come, sir, your 'passado'.
[They fight]</td><td>sword thrust</td></tr>
<tr><td>ROMEO</td><td>Draw, Benvolio, beat down their weapons.
Gentlemen, for shame forbear this outrage!
Tybalt, Mercutio, the Prince expressly hath
Forbid this bandying in Verona streets.</td><td>criminal behaviour
brawling</td></tr>
<tr><td>30</td><td>[He steps between the fighting Mercutio and Tybalt]
Hold Tybalt! Good Mercutio!
[Tybalt thrusts his sword into Mercutio under Romeo's arm. Tybalt flees]</td><td></td></tr>
<tr><td>MERCUTIO</td><td>I am hurt;
A plague on both your houses! I am sped.
Is he gone and hath nothing?
What, art thou hurt?</td><td>families; killed</td></tr>
<tr><td>BENVOLIO
MERCUTIO</td><td>Ay, ay, a scratch, a scratch, marry, 'tis enough.
Where is my page? Go villain, fetch a surgeon.
[Exit Page]</td><td>fellow</td></tr>
<tr><td>ROMEO
MERCUTIO
40</td><td>Courage, man, the hurt cannot be much.
No, 'tis not so deep as a well, nor so wide as a church-door, but 'tis enough, 'twill serve. Ask for me tomorrow, and you shall find me a grave man.
I am peppered, I warrant, for this world. A plague on both your houses!</td><td></td></tr>
</table>

In dialogue, each time a character speaks, what they say is called a speech.

▷▷ STARTING POINTS

- Examples of dialogue you have seen and heard on television.

- The death of Mercutio dialogue can be used as your model. Two people are spoiling for a fight, a third person wants to stop it.

- Two young children are quarrelling over who should have a toy. An adult overhears them...

- A thirteen-year-old comes in late, The parents are waiting up...

- A police officer has stopped a speeding motorist. The passenger joins in...

- Two pupils are quarrelling. A teacher approaches...

- The year is 1600. Two Elizabethan men, wearing swords, meet in the street. They are watched by a woman in a nearby window...

▷▷ CLUES FOR SUCCESS

- Begin with two characters. Have a third character intervene in some way.

- Use short sentences and exclamations.

- Each character responds to the other, using their name or a pronoun.

- Ensure that conflict begins the scene and runs through it.

- End the dialogue with especially dramatic language.

>> **WRITING FRAME**

MARY John! Why .... ?
JOHN I ....
MARY You ....
JOHN No! You ....

and so on...
Then introduce a third character...

MARY We ....
LEENA Let's ....
JOHN You ....
LEENA Please! I ....
MARY You ....

and so on to a dramatic ending.

>> **REDRAFTING AND IMPROVING**

In groups, or with another student, take parts and speak the dialogue you have written. Then share ideas about how your dialogue might be improved to make it more dramatic.

- Does each character have a clear motive for speaking?
- Do characters respond to what other characters say?
- Are actions suggested in the language?
- Does the dialogue build up to a climax and end dramatically?

6 > Looking back

- **Dialogue** is characters speaking, listening and responding to each other.
- **Conflict** of some kind is always present.
- The language contains clues for action.
- Dialogue reveals each character's **point of view**, their **motives**, thoughts and feelings.

Shakespeare's verse

1 ▶ **Purpose**

In this unit you will:
- read two examples of Shakespeare's verse
- learn about the language of Shakespeare's verse
- explore ways of speaking the rhythm of the verse
- write in the verse style of Shakespeare

2 ▶ **O lovely wall!**

In A Midsummer Night's Dream, *Bottom the weaver is acting the part of Pyramus, who hopes to meet his true love, Thisbe. He is on stage with Snout the tinker who plays Wall. Bottom is determined to put on a great show for the audience!*

O grim-looked night, O night with **hue** so black,   *colour*
O night which ever art when day is not!
O night, O night, alack, alack, alack,
I fear my Thisbe's promise is forgot!
5 And thou, O wall, O sweet, O lovely wall,
That stand'st between her father's ground and mine,
Thou wall, O wall, O sweet and lovely wall,
Show me thy chink, to blink through with mine eyne.
[Wall parts his fingers]
Thanks, courteous wall; **Jove** shield thee well for this!
                        King (of the Gods)
10 But what see I? No Thisbe do I see.
O wicked wall, through whom I see no bliss,
Cursed be thy stones for thus deceiving me!

3 ▸ Key features

Shakespeare's verse:

● looks like poetry

● is set out in lines, each beginning with a capital letter

● each line has a 'five-beat' rhythm:
ti-TUM ti-TUM ti-TUM ti-TUM ti-TUM

≫ ● To which two things does Bottom speak?
● How do Bottom's feelings towards Wall change?
● Does each line have a 'five-beat' rhythm?

4 ▷ Language skills

Word

The English language has changed since Shakespeare's time. In line 2, *art* is the **old word** for *are*.

❶ What old words does Bottom use for 'eye' (line 8) and 'alas'?

Bottom's use of O is an example of **apostrophe**, an address to a person or object:

> *O night   O wall*

You probably know two other meanings of apostrophe:

- the mark (') that you use to show possession: *Thisbe's = promise of Thisbe*
- that a letter is missing in a word: *stand'st* = standest

Apostrophe adds to the humour of Bottom's speech because it seems ridiculous for him to address night and wall. Today, apostrophe is hardly ever used except in prayers or in fun.

❷ Try using *O* to address a friend (*O Susan, O John*) or an object (*O table, O pencil*). What is the effect of using such a way of addressing somebody or something?

❸ Write two lines of verse that contain at least one apostrophe in the way that Bottom uses it. You could have a teacher addressing a piece of chalk or you addressing your lunch.

Sentence

In Shakespeare's **verse**, each **line** has a 'five-beat' **rhythm**:

> *ti-TUM ti-TUM ti-TUM ti-TUM ti-TUM*

Shakespeare wants to make the audience laugh at Bottom's speech, so he deliberately exaggerates the rhythm of his verse:

> *O **grim**-looked **night**, O **night** with **hue** so **black**,*
> *O **night** which **ever art** when **day** is **not**!... and so on.*

❶ Speak Bottom's speech, bringing out the 'five-beat' rhythm of each line.

- Clap your hands or tap the desk to emphasise the five beats.

- Work with a partner: link hands and move in time to the rhythm.

- Test how the verse rhythm helps your memory! Speak the first line as rhythmically as you can, emphasising the five 'beats'. Then close your eyes and speak the line aloud from memory. Use the rhythm to help you learn the whole speech.

Lines 5–8 are a single sentence, but because the sentence is written as **verse**, each line begins with a **capital letter**. In **prose** (continuous writing), only the first word of a sentence has a capital letter.

❷ Write out lines 5–8 as prose. Which words which have capital letters in verse do not now have capitals in your prose?

Text

Bottom's speech is in rhyme, but Shakespeare wrote mainly in **blank verse**: unrhymed verse. Here is an example of blank verse from *Richard III* in which Richard's brother, Clarence, tells of his terrible dream that he was drowning.

Clarence's dream

O Lord, methought what pain it was to drown!
What dreadful noise of waters in my ears!
What sights of ugly death within my eyes!
Methought I saw a thousand fearful **wracks**;   *wrecks*
5 A thousand men that fishes gnawed upon;
Wedges of gold, great anchors, heaps of pearls,
Inestimable stones, unvalued jewels,   *uncountable diamonds*
All scattered in the bottom of the sea.
Some lay in dead men's skulls, and in the holes
10 Where eyes did once inhabit, there were crept
As 'twere in **scorn** of eyes, reflecting gems,   *mocking imitation*
That woo'd the slimy bottom of the **deep**,   *ocean*
And mock'd the dead bones that lay scatt'red by.

❶ Speak the lines aloud, using the 'five-beat' rhythm to help you

> O **Lord**, me**thought** what **pain** it **was** to **drown**

When you speak the verse in a 'five-beat' rhythm, there is a danger that it sounds like clockwork, very regular and mechanical. But Shakespeare wrote his plays to be enjoyed, not to sound monotonous and boring. His verse is **dramatic language**, written to be spoken on stage, full of **meaning and emotion**. That means that every actor will take account of the rhythm, but will not speak it regularly.

So don't worry if it was difficult to find the 'five-beat' rhythm in some lines. For example, line 7 *Inestimable stones*, *unvalued jewels* can fit the rhythm – but no-one would speak it like that on stage!

❷ Work on your own or with another student and prepare a spoken presentation of Clarence's lines as dramatically as possible.

5 ▶ Planning your own writing

Write your own verse in Shakespeare's style:

Either: telling of a dream you had. Use Clarence's dream to help you

Or: a speech for Bottom, to follow his 'Wall' speech, in which he finally meets Thisbe.

Use the writing frames provided, but you can ignore them if you wish and make up your own beginnings.

▶▶ STARTING POINT

- Remind yourself of the rhythm by saying, and tapping out:

  ti-TUM ti-TUM ti-TUM ti-TUM ti-TUM

- Then try making up a few single lines in that rhythm:

  I'd **like** to **have** a **plate** of **fish** and **chips**
  or
  My **birth**day **is** the **twen**ty-**third** of **May**

- Next, try making up two or four lines that are a single sentence:

  Today I'll try to make my teacher smile,
  By writing verse in Willy Shakespeare's style.

IAMBIC PENTAMETER

- The technical term for Shakespeare's 'five-beat' rhythm is *iambic pentameter*. Don't feel afraid of that formal sounding label. Here's how it's made up:

- *iamb* (*Latin* for *foot*) is two syllables, the first unstressed or short, the second stressed or long, for example a**lack**, win**ter**, a**like**. The iamb is a natural rhythm because it is like the human heartbeat. Listen to the rhythm of your heart, or feel your pulse – you can hear it beating ti-TUM, ti-TUM, Ti-TUM........

- *penta* is from the Greek for five, and *meter* means a rhythmical verse pattern

- so *iambic pentameter* means a line with a 'five-beat' rhythm:
  A thousand men that fishes gnawed upon.

 **CLUES FOR SUCCESS**

- Begin each line with a capital letter.
- Speak your lines aloud.
- Tap out the 'five-beat' rhythm.
- Choose whether to write in rhyme, or in blank verse (unrhymed).

>> **REDRAFTING AND IMPROVING**

Improve your own verse writing by:

- changing words to make each line more rhythmical
- checking spelling and punctuation
- using language that will entertain an audience

>> **WRITING FRAMES**

Bottom meets Thisbe
O _____ _____ _____, O _____ with _____ so _____,
Where is my Thisbe, _____ _____ _____ _____ _____?
I'll search the _____, and look in every _____,
To find my love, and fill my _____ with _____!
But what is this? _____ _____ _____ _____ _____ carry on!

My dream
Last night I had the very strangest dream,
Of _____, and _____, and even _____ _____ _____.
I'll tell you all that happened in my head
As I _____ _____ …carry on!

6 > **Looking back**

- Shakespeare's verse can be **rhymed** or **unrhymed** (blank verse)
- Each line has the rhythm: ti-TUM ti-TUM ti-TUM ti-TUM ti-TUM
- The verse is not regular like the ticking of a clock. That would make it boring to speak or listen to.
- Shakespeare's verse is dramatic language – written to entertain the audience. So speak it to bring out the mood and meaning – and the humour!

Prose

In this unit you will:
- read an example of Shakespeare's prose
- learn about scenes written in prose to be performed on stage
- write your own prose to be acted out

2 > Strange bedfellows

In The Tempest, *the jester Trinculo has been shipwrecked on an island. He fears a storm is coming and looks for shelter. He finds a strange figure lying under a cloak. Who is it? What is it? He decides to seek shelter under the cloak.*

Here's neither bush nor shrub to **bear off** any weather at *shelter from*
all. And another storm brewing. I hear it sing i'th'wind.
Yond same black cloud, yond huge one, looks like a foul
bombard that would shed his liquor. If it should thunder *large leather bottle*
5 as it did before, I know not where to hide my head. Yond
same cloud cannot choose but fall by pailfuls.

What have we here? A man or a fish? Dead or alive? A
fish, he smells like a fish; a very ancient and fishlike smell;
a kind of not-of-the-newest **poor-John**. A strange fish! *salted fish*
10 Were I in England now (as once I was) and had but this
fish **painted**, not a holiday fool there but would give a *advertised on a board*
piece of silver. There would this monster make a man.
Any strange beast there makes a man. When they will not
give a **doit** to relieve a lame beggar, they will lay out *small coin*
15 ten to see a dead Indian.

68

Legged like a man; and his fins like arms! Warm, **o'my troth**! I do now let loose my opinion, hold it no longer: this is no fish, but an islander that hath lately suffered by a thunderbolt.

by my faith

20   Alas, the storm is come again! My best way is to creep under his **gaberdine**. There is no other shelter hereabout. Misery acquaints a man with strange bedfellows. I will shroud here till the **dregs** of the storm be past.

cloak

last drops

3 ❯ Key features

Prose is language that is not arranged in lines of verse like poetry. It is normal, continuous writing.

In this scene, Trinculo's prose:

- uses short sentences
- contains many nouns
- explores and resolves problems
- moves from thought to thought

In Shakespeare's plays, prose is used mainly by comic characters, low status characters or characters pretending to be mad.

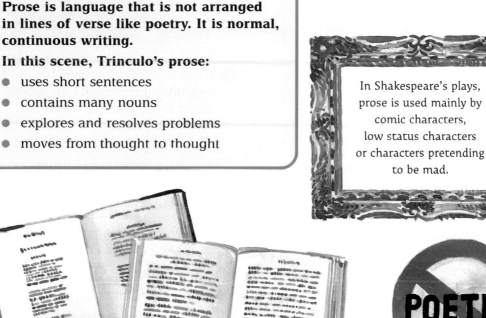

Poetry

Prose

Prose is language that is not poetry

- Where does the scene take place?
- How do you know the language is in prose?
- What does Trinculo finally decide to do?

4 ❭ Language skills

Word

Trinculo uses many **nouns** which give a rich impression of the island, the storm, and what he sees. His language includes:

common nouns – a label for people, things or animals, for example *bush*, *shrub*, *cloud*

abstract nouns – a label for things we cannot touch such as ideas or emotions, for example *smell*, *opinion*

1 Write down a list of all the nouns that Trinculo uses.

2 Divide up your list of nouns into three columns: proper nouns, abstract nouns and words which could be either common nouns or abstract nouns (such as *weather*). Write a brief note next to the words in the third column, explaining why you think that they could be either common nouns or abstract nouns.

3 Some nouns are unusual, because they are old words, and have dropped out of use since Shakespeare's day (*bombard*, *poor-John*, *doit*, *troth*). The meanings are given alongside the text. Invent a noun of your own you could put in place of the unusual word, if you were performing the play at school. Write down your invented nouns.

Sentence

Trinculo is a jester, and his role in the play is to make the audience laugh. Actors often do this by emphasising one particular word. For example, the sentence *And another storm brewing* could be spoken as:

   ***And** another storm brewing*
or *And **another** storm brewing*
or *And another **storm** brewing*
or *And another storm* (long pause) ***brewing!***

1 Read through the speech, identifying the words an actor could emphasise to make the audience laugh.

Shakespeare sometimes includes long **adjectival phrases** to add comic detail. For example, in lines 8–9 he describes a smell as *a very ancient and fish-like smell*; and a fish as *a kind of not-of-the-newest poor John*.

2 In the sentence that begins *A fish, he smells like a fish*, add two or three of your own invented adjectival phrases to the noun 'fish' that help build up the comedy.

Because this is **dramatic language**, each sentence contains at least one clue as to what the actor might do (actions, facial expressions etc.) to accompany the words.

3 Write notes suggesting what Trinculo might do as he speaks each sentence.

Trinculo's thoughts shift with every sentence. He uses **statements**, **questions** and **exclamations**. As he discovers more about the creature beneath the *gaberdine* (cloak) he begins to think about how he might make money from it, by exhibiting it in England.

4 Consider every sentence in turn. Write one or two words that express his meaning or mood in each sentence. To start you off:

sentence 1 No shelter!
sentence 2 More thunder!
sentence 3 Listen!
sentence 4 Rain coming!

Text

Trinculo's prose is **colloquial**: its words and style are like everyday informal speech. His language is like that used in **conversations** at the time when Shakespeare lived, and most of it is still very familiar. Because his speech is like a conversation, the actor playing Trinculo can choose whether he talks to himself or sometimes to the audience.

1 Consider each sentence in turn and suggest whether Trinculo says it to himself or to the audience. Give a reason for your decision about each sentence

Trinculo's prose is set out in four **paragraphs**: blocks of sentences all about one main idea or subject. The paragraphs show the **structure** of Trinculo's speech:

● the storm

● his first thoughts about what is under the gaberdine, and how he might profit from it

● more thoughts on his guess about what it is

● the storm: what to do?

2 Rewrite the first sentence of each paragraph. Use different words, but express the same meaning. And remember, your aim is to make the audience laugh!

5 ▶ Planning your own writing

Write a prose speech for a character to deliver on stage. Your intention is that the language will make the audience laugh.

▶▶ STARTING POINTS

Invent a character and a situation. Here are a few that might help you.

- A tramp stumbles across a gold mine.

- An office cleaner finds an open safe filled with cash.

- A man, looking for his socks, makes a curious discovery.

- A school pupil, searching for a book in the library, comes across something unexpected.

▶▶ CLUES FOR SUCCESS

- Use short sentences.

- Ask questions, use exclamations.

- Include clues for action in each sentence.

- Use plenty of nouns to increase the detail of descriptions.

- Let your character 'wander off', speculating (guessing) about what they have discovered.

- Use a clear structure, so that your speech has three or four paragraphs.

▶▶ WRITING FRAMES

You might find it helpful to use the following structure:

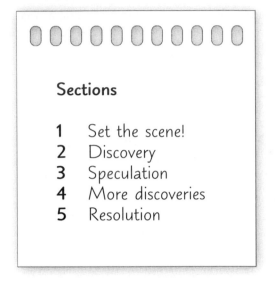

Sections

1 Set the scene!
2 Discovery
3 Speculation
4 More discoveries
5 Resolution

▶▶ REDRAFTING AND IMPROVING

Work with another student or in groups and look closely at your own and other people's first drafts. Make suggestions for improving or adding more detail. Then think about how your own writing can be made more dramatically effective, for example:

- Does the language show what the character is like?

- Can new or different common nouns or abstract nouns add to the atmosphere you create?

Example	Language features
What a strange strange place!	exclamation, nouns
But what's this?	question, nouns
If I were in...	first person (I)
Now look at this!...	exclamation, nouns
This is what to do...	

- Does each short sentence build on the thought of the previous sentence?

- Is the structure of the speech clear? Are there dramatic beginnings to each section?

6 Looking back

- **Prose** is language that is not poetry.

- Prose is often **colloquial**, using vocabulary and expressions close to everyday informal speech.

- Thoughts, moods and feelings change throughout a prose speech.

Sonnets

1 ▷ Purpose

In this unit you will:
- read Shakespeare's Sonnet 18
- learn about the language of Shakespeare's sonnets
- write your own sonnet

3 ▷ Key features

- each Shakespeare sonnet has 14 lines
- each line has a 'five-beat' rhythm: ti-TUM ti-TUM ti-TUM ti-TUM ti-TUM
- the first 12 lines rhyme alternately
- the last 2 lines rhyme together

>> • Does this sonnet have 14 lines?
  • What do the last two lines say?
  • Suggest a title for the sonnet.

2 Sonnet 18

Shall I compare thee to a summer's day?

Shall I compare thee to a summer's day?

Thou art more lovely and more **temperate**;   calm, even-tempered

Rough winds do shake the darling buds of May,

4   And summer's lease hath all too short a date.

Sometime too hot the **eye of heaven** shines,   sun

And often is his gold complexion dimmed,

And every **fair** from fair sometime declines,   beautiful person or thing

8   By chance or nature's changing course **untrimmed**.   robbed of beauty

But thy eternal summer shall not fade,

Nor lose possession of that fair thou **ow'st**,   own, possess

Nor shall death brag thou wander'st in his shade,

12   When in **eternal lines** to time thou grow'st.   immortal poetry

So long as men can breathe, or eyes can see,

So long lives **this**, and this gives life to thee.   this sonnet

4 ▸ Language skills

Word

Shakespeare's sonnets always use **imagery**, emotionally charged words and phrases that conjure up vivid mental pictures in the imagination:

eye of heaven – an image for the sun

fair – for a beautiful person or thing

summer's lease – an image of summer renting or borrowing a few months from the year.

1 Write down a list of all the images you can find in Sonnet 18.

2 Invent some images of your own for the sun, a beautiful person, summer, a sonnet. Write them down.

Shakespeare uses **old words** which are not in use today, like *thee*, *thou* and *thy* for *you* and *your*. He also uses **unfamiliar** or **unexpected words** for poetic effect, like *darling buds of May*.

3 Why do you think Shakespeare uses the word *darling*? Write down two or three possible meanings of *darling buds of May*. It will help to look up *darling* in a thesaurus, where you will find words with connected meanings.

4 Write down the old words in the sonnet and words that you find unfamiliar or surprising. Then imagine you are Shakespeare, writing the sonnet today. Will you change any of those words? Explain why or why not.

Sentence

In a Shakespeare sonnet, each **line** usually makes sense on its own, even if it is part of a longer sentence.

1 Read the sonnet a line at a time, pausing at the end of each line. In each pause, write the meaning of the line in your own words.

Sometimes Shakespeare writes a sentence in **monosyllables**: single syllable words which can be given added emphasis when the sentence is spoken aloud.

2 Which sentence in the sonnet is made up only of monosyllables? Suggest a reason why Shakespeare uses short simple words in this particular sentence.

3 Write a sentence, all in monosyllables, saying what you think of Shakespeare. *Shakespeare* has two syllables, so you can call him Bill the Bard or some other monosyllabic name!

The sonnet begins with a **question**, and then makes many **statements**: expressions of fact or opinion. All the statements are intended to prove that the beloved person to whom the sonnet is addressed is more beautiful than a summer's day.

4 How many statements can you find? How many describe *a summer's day*?

Text

The **structure** of a Shakespeare sonnet is 14 lines arranged in 4 sections: 3 **stanzas** (or **quatrains**) and a **couplet**:

lines 1–4   first stanza (4 lines)
lines 5–8   second stanza (4 lines)
lines 9–12   third stanza (4 lines)
lines 13–14   couplet (2 lines)

It is helpful to think of each stanza as a **paragraph**, expressing a particular thought, and the couplet as a kind of 'sting in the tail' or summary.

1 Read the first stanza (lines 1–4), and summarise what it says as briefly as you can. Then do the same for the second and third stanzas and the couplet. Notice how each makes a separate, but related, point.

Each line has a 'five-beat' **rhythm**:
ti-TUM ti-TUM ti-TUM ti-TUM ti-TUM

(this rhythm or **metre** is called **iambic pentameter** – see page 66)

2 Check that each line has a five beat rhythm by tapping out the five stresses as you speak the line.

The **rhyme scheme** of a Shakespeare sonnet is: lines 1–12 rhyme alternately; line 13 rhymes with 14.

3 Speak aloud only the word at the end of each line. Which lines rhyme with which?

Sonnets can be written on any **theme** or **topic**. It is a short poem which tells a story or explores a thought or experience. For example, although all of Shakespeare's 154 sonnets are about love, he sometimes places a sonnet in a play for a different purpose. At the beginning of *Romeo and Juliet* he uses a sonnet to tell the audience the story of the play.

4 Write down your answers to each of these two questions: How would you describe the theme or topic of Sonnet 18? If you had to give a title to Sonnet 18, what would your title be?

5 Try reading the sonnet giving increasing emphasis to each line, as if you had more and more conviction about the truth of what you are saying as you pile up statement upon statement. With another student, decide whether the sonnet should be read like that and explain your reasons

5 > Planning your own writing

Here's a sonnet to help you write your own sonnet. Read it aloud and you will find that each line has the familiar 'five-beat' Shakespearean rhythm. You will also discover that it is arranged as three stanzas followed by a couplet.

> You want to write a Shakespeare sonnet? Fine!
> The rules are few, the skill will quickly come.
> Remember first the rhythm of each line:
> Ti-TUM ti-TUM ti-TUM ti-TUM ti-TUM.
>
> You've fourteen lines in which to write your verse,
> Made up of 4 + 4 + 4 + 2;
> Each 4 is called a 'stanza' – nothing worse,
> The 2's a 'couplet' – Is this helping you?
>
> Lines 1 to 12 have alternating rhymes,
> Line 1 with 3, line 2 with 4, – like that;
> The couplet rhymes itself, like 'dimes' with 'times',
> Its two lines often knock the reader flat!
>
> So now you know just how to write a sonnet,
> Make up your own, with Shakespeare's marks upon it.

>> STARTING POINT

- Choose a topic: something that really interests you. It might be football or pop music or animals – anything – even Shakespeare!

- Think of just one thing you really want to say about your chosen topic

- Write the first stanza in sonnet style

>> CLUES FOR SUCCESS

- Think about the tone of your sonnet. Is it serious or funny?

- Speak each line aloud to ensure it has a 'five-beat' rhythm

- Work in 4 line units (stanzas).

- Check your rhymes to make sure they fit the pattern.

- Make sure the couplet really grabs the reader's attention!

⟫ WRITING FRAMES

- **First lines** — Here are some first lines you may wish to use:
  I'll tell you of the finest football team, *or*
  I have the strangest cat in all the world, *or*
  One pop star stands quite clear of all the rest

- **Your own version of Sonnet 18** — Use sonnet 18 to make your own comparisons:
  Shall I compare thee to a (TUM ti-TUM)?
  Make sure your comparison has the same rhythm as *summer's day*, for example
  hard boiled egg   TV soap   dinosaur

- **Rhymes**
  Think of rhymes you enjoy, and build your sonnet around them!
  Can you think of a rhyme for *dinosaur*? (*lino floor*?)

⟫ REDRAFTING AND IMPROVING

When you have written a first draft, work with a partner. Read each other's sonnets.

Can you make improvements by:

- correcting spellings or punctuations?
- changing words to make them more imaginative?
- changing words to ensure that each line has a 'five-beat' rhythm?
- making the couplet more of 'a sting in the tail'?

Now write your final version. You might word process it to put on display for others to read.

6 ⟫ Looking back

When you have written your sonnet, read it and check:

- Does it have 14 lines?
- Does each line have a 'five-beat' rhythm?
- Does it rhyme appropriately?
- Will the **couplet** surprise and delight the reader?

Glossary

Adjectives are words which help to give more information about a noun or pronoun.

Alliteration is the repetition of consonants, usually at the beginning of words.

Apostrophe can be either a punctuation mark (') that shows possession (William's), or shows that a letter or several letters have been missed out (e'en = even), or an exclamation (O), made by a person addressing an object or idea: O wall!

Blank verse is unrhymed verse written in iambic pentameter.

Colloquial language is a style of speaking or writing that is informal and familiar. It contrasts with literary language.

Conjunctions are words used to join parts of a sentence, phrases or single words, for example *and*, *but*, *if*.

Couplets are two lines of verse, often rhyming, usually at the end of a speech or sonnet.

Iambic pentameter is the 'five-beat' rhythm of a line of Shakespeare's verse:
ti-TUM ti-TUM ti-TUM ti-TUM ti-TUM.

Imagery is the use of emotionally-charged words to conjure up vivid pictures in the imagination. Imagery uses metaphor, simile and personification.

Imperative is the form of a verb used to express commands.

Line is the basic unit of Shakespeare's verse. Each line begins with a capital letter.

Metaphor is a comparison of two things that does not use *like* or *as*.

Monosyllable is a word of only one syllable.

Nouns are the words in a sentence which label a person, thing, feeling or idea.

Onomatopoeia is when a word has a sound which echoes its meaning, such as *crash* or *bang*.

Palindromic sentence is one that reads the same forwards and backwards: Fair is foul and foul is fair.

Parody is a mocking imitation of a particular style of language.

Personification is a special kind of metaphor in which an object or idea is described as if it were a person.

Pronouns are words which can be used in place of a noun, for example *I*, *she*, *they*, *we*, *it*.

Rhyme is the effect produced by using words which end with the same or similar sounds.

Rhyme scheme is the pattern of rhymes in a poem.

Simile is a comparison that uses *like* or *as*.

Soliloquy is a speech by a character who is alone on stage (or thinks he or she is alone).

Stage directions are instructions to actors, often written in italics, in the script of a play.

Stanza is a section of a poem. In a sonnet, a stanza is a unit of four lines.

Verbs are words in a sentence that help you say what people or things are doing.